To Doris

KU-470-579

Jyoti
a.

The Pieta Prayer Book

Michael Gabriel

Copyright © 2017 Michael Gabriel

All rights reserved.

ISBN: 9781549815638

TO THE READER

This booklet on prayer is an effort to apply the scientific method to the Truths of our Roman Catholic Faith; to obtain more grace to better serve God, drawing particularly on that gigantic source of God's **Infinite Goodness and Mercy** - a source virtually untapped - **PROPHETIC REVELATIONS.**

CONTENTS

ACKNOWLEDGMENTS

The Blessed Virgin said: "You love Me and make others love Me." This revised edition of the Pieta Prayer Book is dedicated to Thee Dear Lady of Ephesus as an act of love to honor thine Assumption. "I am all thine my Queen and Mother and all that I have is Thine,"

1. PURPOSE

Scripture says: "Pray without ceasing." St. Paul of the Cross wrote: "We enter on the broad road of perdition when we neglect prayer." Dr. Alexis Carrel wrote: "If you make a habit of prayer, your life will be profoundly altered." As a scientist, he turned to prayer as man s highest activity; that conversation with God to be an art of all arts.

May this Pieta Prayer Booklet serve as a spiritual tool for souls who wish to increase their daily prayer life. May the Dear Angels who carried the Holy House of Loreto carry this booklet to all persons who wish to pray more after reciting the daily rosary.

The Pieta Prayer Book includes:

15 prayers of Saint Bridget, Ave Maris Stella, To the Blessed Virgin, To Saint Joseph, Glory Be to Jesus and Mary, Prayer for Daily Neglects, Hail Mary of Gold , Three Very Beautiful Prayers, Act of Contrition, Tips on Prayer, Prayer to Obtain the Grace of all World's Masses, Graces Derived from Assisting at Mass, Holy Communion, True Letter of Our Savior Jesus Christ, Prayer to the Infant of Prague, Prayers after Mass and Communion, Devotions and Prayers, The Rosary and Scapular, Why Daily Mass?, Short Way of The Cross, Prayer to the Shoulder Wound of Christ, Honor the Holy Wounds of Jesus Christ, Pray for Souls in Purgatory, The Spiritual Communion, Message of Worldwide Importance, Prayer or Blessing Against Storms, The Angelus and St. Michael Prayer, Chaplet of Saint Michael, Salve Regina, Daily Prayer to Guardian Angel, Saint Therese, The Golden Arrow, Consecration to Jesus Christ, Catena Legionis, The Priesthood, Litany of Humility, Prayers to The Sacred Head, Efficacious Novena to Sacred Heart, Last Two Hours of Our Life.

St. Birgitta of Sweden (1303-1373)
A Woman who changed the world
A saint of our time

BRIDE OF CHRIST

"Birgitta, I am speaking not only to you but to all Christians. You will be MY bride... and it shall be through you that I will speak to the world. My Spirit will dwell in you until your death."

2. The Fifteen Prayers of Saint Bridget of Sweden

These prayers were revealed by Our Lord to Saint Bridget in the Church of St. Paul at Rome, and are published under sanction of the Decree of November 18, 1966, published in the Acta of Apostolicae Sadism, Vol. 58, No. 16 of December 29, 1966.

The prayers have been approved by Pope Pius IX, and Pope Benedict XV expressed himself as follows on the Revelations of St. Bridget:

"The approbation of such revelations implies nothing more than, after mature examination, it is permissible to publish them for the unit of the faithful. Though they don't merit the same credence as the truths of religion, one can, however, believe them out of human faith, conforming to the rules of prudence by which they are probable, and supported by sufficient motives that one might believe in them piously." (Les Petits Bollandistes, tome XII)

The 14th of June 1303, at the moment Bridget was born, Benedict, the curate of Rasbo, prayed for the happy deliverance of Ingeborde. Suddenly, he found himself enveloped by a luminous cloud out of which Our Lady appeared:

"A child has been born at Birger; her voice will be heard by the entire world." Sagii, die XXIV Aprilis 1903

Imprimatur

F. J. GIRARD, V. G.

These Prayers and these Promises have been copied from a book printed in Toulouse in 1740 and published by the P. Adrien Parvilliers of the Company of Jesus, Apostolic Missionary of the Holy Land, with approbation, permission and recommendation to distribute them.

Parents and teachers who will read them to young infants for at least one year will assure their being preserved for life from any grave accident which would involve the loss of one of their five senses.

Pope Pius IX took cognizance of these Prayers with the prologue; he approved them May 31, 1862, recognizing them as true and for the good of souls.

This sentence of Pope Pius IX has been confirmed by the realization of promises by all persons who have recited the prayers and by numerous supernatural facts by which God wanted to make known their exact truth. A collection of small books, these prayers among them, was approved by the Great Congress of Malines on August 22, 1863.

Question -- Must one recite the Prayers every day without interruption to obtain the privileges?

Answer -- One should miss saying them as few times as possible; but if for a serious reason one is obliged to miss them, one doesn't lose the privileges attached to them, as long as one recites 5480 prayers during the year. One must say them with devotion and concentrate on the words one pronounces.

These prayers can serve as the Way of the Cross.

Visitors to the Church of St. Paul at Rome can see the crucifix, above the Tabernacle in the Blessed Sacrament Chapel, sculptured by Pierre Cavallini, before which St. Bridget knelt when she received these 15 Prayers from Our Lord. The following inscription is placed in the church to commemorate the event: "Pendentis, Pendente Dei verba accepit aure accipit et verbum corde Brigitta Deum. Anno Jubilei MCCCL", which recalls the prodigy with which the crucifix conversed with Bridget.

As St. Bridget for a long time wanted to know **the number of blows Our Lord received during His Passion**, He one day appeared to her and said: "I received **5480 blows on My Body**. If you wish to honor them in some way, recite fifteen times the Our Father and Hail Mary, together with the following prayers, which I Myself will teach you for an entire year. When the year is finished, you will have honored each of My Wounds."

Our Lord made the following promises to anyone who recited the fifteen Saint Bridget Prayers devoutly every day for a whole year:

Promises

1. I will deliver 15 souls of his lineage from Purgatory.
2. 15 souls of his lineage will be confirmed and preserved in grace.
3. 15 sinners of his lineage will be converted.
4. Whoever recites these Prayers will attain the first degree of perfection.
5. 15 days before his death, I will give him My Precious Body in order that he may escape eternal starvation; I will give him my Precious Blood to drink lest he thirst eternally.
6. 15 days before his death he will feel a deep contrition for all his sins and will have a perfect knowledge of them.
7. I will place before him the sign of My Victorious Cross for his help and defense against the attacks of his enemies.
8. Before his death I shall come with My Dearest Beloved Mother.

9. I shall graciously receive his soul, and will lead it into eternal joys.
10. And having led it there I shall give him a special draught from the fountain of My Deity, something I will not do for those who have not recited My Prayers.
11. Let it be known that whoever may have been living in a state of mortal sin for 30 years, but who will recite devoutly, or have the intention to recite these Prayers, I the Lord will forgive him all his sins.
12. I shall protect him from strong temptations.
13. I shall preserve and guard his five senses.
14. I shall preserve him from a sudden death.
15. His soul will be delivered from eternal death.
16. He will obtain all he asks for from God and the Blessed Virgin.
17. If he has lived all his life doing his own will and he is to die the next day, his life will be prolonged.
18. Every time one recites these Prayers he gains 100 days indulgence.
19. He is assured of being joined to the supreme Choir of Angels.
20. Whoever teaches these prayers to another will have continual joy and merit which will last throughout eternity.
21. There where these Prayers are being said or will be said in the future, God is present with His grace.

First Prayer: Our Father - Hail Mary

O Jesus Christ! Eternal Sweetness to those who love Thee, joy surpassing all joy and all desire, Salvation and Hope of all sinners, who hast proved that Thou hast no greater desire than to be among men, even assuming human nature at the fullness of time for the love of men, recall all the sufferings Thou hast endured from the instant of Thy conception, and especially during Thy Passion, as it was decreed and ordained from eternity in the Divine plan.

Remember, O Lord, that during the Last Supper with Thy disciples having washed their feet, thou gavest them Thy Most Precious Body and Blood, and while at the same time Thou didst sweetly console them, Thou didst foretell them Thy Coming Passion.

Remember the sadness and bitterness which Thou didst experience in Thy Soul as Thou Thyself bore witness saying: "*My Soul is sorrowful even unto death.*"

Remember all the fear, anguish and pain that Thou didst suffer in Thy Delicate Body before the torment of the Crucifixion, when, after having prayed three times, bathed in a sweat of blood, thou were betrayed by Judas, thy disciple, arrested by the people of a nation Thou hadst chosen and elevated, accused by false witnesses, unjustly judged by three judges during the flower of Thy youth and during the solemn Paschal season.

Remember that Thou was despoiled of Thy garments and clothed in those of derision; that Thy Face and Eyes were veiled, that Thou was buffeted, crowned with thorns, a reed placed in Thy Hands, that Thou was crushed with blows and overwhelmed with affronts and outrages.

In memory of all these pains and sufferings which Thou didst endure before Thy Passion on the Cross, grant me before my death true contrition, a sincere and entire confession, worthy satisfaction and the remission all my sins. Amen.

Second Prayer: Our Father -- Hail Mary

O Jesus! True liberty of angels, paradise of delights, remember the horror and sadness which Thou didst endure when Thy enemies, like furious lions, surrounded Thee, and by thousands of insults, spits, blows, lacerations and other unheard-of cruelties, tormented Thee at will. In consideration of these torments and insulting words, I beseech Thee, O my Savior, to deliver me from all my enemies, visible and invisible, and to bring me, under Thy protection, to the perfection of eternal salvation. Amen.

Third Prayer: Our Father -- Hail Mary

O Jesus! Creator of Heaven and earth Whom nothing can encompass or limit, Thou Who dost enfold and hold all under Thy loving power, remember the very bitter pain Thou didst suffer when the Jews nailed Thy Sacred Hands and Feet to the Cross by blow after blow with big blunt nails, and not finding Thee in a pitiable enough state to satisfy their rage, they enlarged thy Wounds, and added pain to pain, and with indescribable cruelty stretched Thy Body on the Cross, pulling Thee from all sides, thus dislocating Thy limbs. I beg of Thee, O Jesus, by the memory of this most Loving suffering of the Cross, to grant me the grace to fear Thee and to Love Thee. Amen.

Fourth Prayer: Our Father -- Hail Mary

O Jesus! Heavenly Physician, raised aloft on the Cross to heal our wounds with Thine, remember the bruises which Thou didst suffer and the weakness of all Thy Members which were distended to such a degree that never was there pain like unto Thine. From the crown of Thy Head to the Soles of Thy Feet there was not one spot on Thy Body that was not in torment, and yet, forgetting all Thy sufferings, thou didst not cease to pray to Thy Heavenly Father for Thy enemies, saying: *"Father forgive them for they know not what they do."*

Through this great Mercy, and in memory of this suffering, grant that the remembrance of Thy Most Bitter Passion may affect in us a perfect contrition and the remission of all our sins. Amen.

Fifth Prayer: Our Father -- Hail Mary

O Jesus! Mirror of eternal splendor, remember the sadness which Thou experienced, when contemplating in the light of Thy Divinity the predestination of those who would be saved by the merits of Thy Sacred Passion, thou didst see at the same time, the great multitude of reprobates who would be damned for their sins, and Thou didst complain bitterly of those hopeless, lost, and unfortunate sinners.

Through this abyss of compassion and pity, and especially through the goodness which Thou displayed to the good thief when Thou saidst to him: "*This day, thou shalt be with Me in Paradise.*" I beg of Thee, O Sweet Jesus, that at the hour of my death, thou wilt show me mercy. Amen.

Sixth Prayer: Our Father -- Hail Mary

O Jesus! Beloved and most desirable King, remember the grief Thou didst suffer, when naked and like a common criminal, thou were fastened and raised on the Cross, when all Thy relatives and friends abandoned Thee, except Thy Beloved Mother, who remained close to Thee during Thy agony and whom Thou didst entrust to Thy faithful disciple when Thou saidst to Mary: "*Woman, behold thy son!*", and to St. John: "*Son, behold thy Mother!*"

I beg of Thee O my Savior, by the sword of sorrow which pierced the soul of Thy Holy Mother, to have compassion on me in all my afflictions and tribulations, both corporal and spiritual, and to assist me in all my trials, and especially at the hour of my death. Amen.

Seventh Prayer: Our Father -- Hail Mary

O Jesus! Inexhaustible Fountain of compassion, who by a profound gesture of Love, said from the Cross: "*I thirst,*" suffered from the thirst for the salvation of the human race.

I beg of Thee, O my Savior, to inflame in our hearts the desire to tend toward perfection in all our acts, and to extinguish in us the concupiscence of the flesh and the ardor of worldly desires. Amen.

Eighth Prayer: Our Father -- Hail Mary

O Jesus! Sweetness of hearts, delight of the spirit, by the bitterness of the gall and vinegar which Thou didst taste on the Cross for Love of us, grant us the grace to receive worthily Thy Precious Body and Blood during our life and at the hour of our death, that they may serve as a remedy and consolation for our souls. Amen.

Ninth Prayer: Our Father -- Hail Mary

O Jesus! Royal virtue, joy of the mind, recall the pain Thou didst endure when plunged in an ocean of bitterness at the approach of death, insulted, outraged by the Jews, thou didst cry out in a loud voice that Thou was abandoned by Thy Father, saying: "*My God, My God, why hast Thou forsaken Me?*"

Through this anguish, I beg of Thee, O my Savior, not to abandon me in the terrors and pains of my death. Amen.

Tenth Prayer: Our Father -- Hail Mary

O Jesus! Who art the beginning and the end of all things, life and virtue, remember that for our sakes Thou was plunged in an abyss of suffering from the soles of Thy Feet to the crown of Thy Head. In consideration of the enormity of Thy Wounds, teach me to keep, through pure love, Thy Commandments, whose way is wide and easy for those who love Thee. Amen.

Eleventh Prayer: Our Father -- Hail Mary

O Jesus! Deep abyss of mercy, I beg of Thee, in memory of Thy Wounds which penetrated to the very marrow of Thy Bones and to the depth of Thy being, to draw me, a miserable sinner, overwhelmed by my offenses, away from sin and to hide me from Thy Face justly irritated against me; hide me in Thy Wounds, until Thy anger and just indignation shall have passed away. Amen.

Twelfth Prayer: Our Father -- Hail Mary

O Jesus! Mirror of truth, symbol of unity, link of charity, remember the multitude of wounds with which Thou was covered from head to foot, torn and reddened by the spilling of Thy Adorable Blood. O great and universal pain which Thou didst suffer in Thy virginal flesh for love of us! Sweetest Jesus! What is there that Thou could have done for us which Thou hast not done?

May the fruit of Thy sufferings be renewed in my soul by the faithful remembrance of Thy Passion, and may Thy love increase in my heart each day until I see Thee in eternity, Thou Who art the treasury of every real good and every joy, which I beg Thee to grant me, O sweetest Jesus, in Heaven. Amen.

Thirteenth Prayer: Our Father -Hail Mary

O Jesus! Strong lion, immortal and invincible King, remember the pain Thou didst endure when all Thy strength, both moral and physical, was entirely exhausted; Thou didst bow Thy Head, saying: "*It is consummated.*"

Through this anguish and grief, I beg of Thee Lord Jesus, to have mercy on me at the hour of my death when my mind will be greatly troubled and my soul will be in anguish. Amen.

Fourteenth Prayer: Our Father-Hail Mary

O Jesus! Only Son of the Father, splendor and figure of His Substance, remember the simple and humble recommendation Thou didst make of Thy Soul to Thy Eternal Father, saying: "*Father, into Thy Hands I commend My Spirit!*" And with Thy Body all torn, and Thy Heart broken, and the bowels of Thy Mercy open to redeem us, thou didst expire.

By this Precious Death, I beg of Thee O King of Saints, to comfort me and help me to resist the devil, the flesh and the world, so that being dead to the world, I may live for Thee alone. I beg of Thee at the hour of my death to receive me, a pilgrim and an exile returning to Thee. Amen.

Fifteenth Prayer: Our Father -- Hail Mary

O Jesus! True and fruitful Vine! Remember the abundant outpouring of blood which Thou didst so generously shed from Thy Sacred Body as juice from grapes in a wine press.

From Thy Side, pierced with a lance by a soldier, blood and water issued forth until there was not left in Thy Body a single drop, and finally, like a bundle of myrrh lifted to the top of the Cross, thy delicate Flesh was destroyed, the very substance of Thy Body withered, and the marrow of Thy Bones dried up.

Through this bitter Passion, and through the outpouring of Thy Precious Blood, I beg of Thee, O Sweet Jesus, to receive my soul when I am in my death agony. Amen.

Conclusion

O Sweet Jesus! Pierce my heart so that my tears of penitence and love will be my bread day and night; may I be converted entirely to Thee, may my heart be Thy perpetual habitation, may my conversation be pleasing to Thee, and may the end of my life be so praiseworthy that I may merit Heaven and there with Thy saints, praise Thee forever. Amen.

3. Promises to those who sing "Ave Maris Stella"

During a riot at Rome, a mob came to the house where St. Bridget lived; a leader talked of burning Bridget alive.
She prayed to Our Lord to know if she should flee to safety. Jesus advised her to stay: "It doesn't matter if they plot thy death. My power will break the malice of thy enemies: If Mine crucified Me, it is because I permitted it." Our Blessed Mother added: "Sing as a group the AVE MARIS STELLA and I'll guard you from every danger."

Ave Maris Stella	Hail thou star of ocean
Dei Mater alma,	Portal of the sky
Atque semper virgo,	Ever virgin Mother
Felix coeli porta.	Of the Lord Most High.
Sumens illud ave	O! by Gabriel's Ave,
Gabrielis ore,	Uttered long ago,
Funda nos in pace,	Eva's name reversing,
Mutans Evae nomen	Established peace below
Solve vincia reis	Break the captives' fetters,
Profer lumen caecis	Light on blindness pour,
Mala nostra pelle,	All our ills expelling,
Bona cuncta posce.	Every bliss implore
Monstra te esse Matrem	Show thyself a Mother,
Sumat per te preces	Offer Him our sighs,
Qui pro nobis natus	Who for us incarnate
Tulit esse tuus	Did not thee despise
Virgo singularis	Virgin of all virgins
Inter omnes mitis	To thy shelter take us,
Nos culpis solutos	Gentlest of the gentle
Mites fac et castos	Chaste and gentle make us

Vitam presta puram	Still, as on we journey,
Iter para tutum,	Help our weak endeavor,
Ut, videntes Jesum	Till with thee and Jesus
Semper collaetemur	We rejoice forever
Sit laus Deo Patri,	through the highest heaven,
Summo Cristo decus	To the almighty Three
Spiritui sancto:	Father, Son, and Spirit,
Tribus honor unus.	One same glory be.
Amen.	Amen.

To the Blessed Virgin

My Queen, my Mother, I give myself entirely to Thee, and to show my devotion to Thee, I consecrate to Thee this day, my eyes, my ears, my mouth, my heart, my whole being without reserve. Wherefore good Mother as I am thine own, keep me, guard me, as thy property and possession. Amen.

"An indulgence of 500 days"

Prayer to St. Joseph over 1900 years old

O   St. Joseph whose protection is so great, so strong, so prompt before the Throne of God, I place in you all my interests and desires. O   St. Joseph do assist me by your powerful intercession and obtain for me from your Divine Son all spiritual blessings through Jesus Christ, Our Lord; so that having engaged here below your Heavenly power I may offer my thanksgiving and homage to the Loving of Fathers. O   St. Joseph, I never weary of contemplating you and Jesus asleep in your arms. I dare not approach you while He reposes near your heart. Press him in my name and kiss His Fine Head for me, and ask Him to return the kiss when I draw my dying breath. St. Joseph, Patron of departing souls, pray for us. Amen.

Say Prayer to St. Joseph for nine consecutive mornings for anything you may desire. It has seldom been known to fail.

This prayer was found in the fiftieth year of Our Lord Jesus Christ. In the 1500's, it was sent by the Pope to Emperor Charles when he was going into battle. Whoever reads this prayer or hears it or carries it, will never die a sudden death, nor be drowned, nor will poison take effect of them. They will not fall into the hands of the enemy nor be burned in any fire, nor will they be defeated in battle. Make this prayer known everywhere.

Imprimatur

Most Rev. George W. Ahr

Bishop of Trenton

Glory Be to Jesus and Mary

A letter written by the Blessed Virgin Mary to the City of Messina where St. Paul, the Apostle preached the gospel, which has been preserved in the Reliquary of the great altar.

"I, Mary Virgin, servant of God, very humble Mother of Jesus Christ, Son of God, the Almighty and Eternity, to all who are in Messina, health and benediction in Our Lord. You have learned by the ambassadors who have been sent to you. You received the gospel and you acknowledged that the Son of God has become man, and has suffered the passion and death for the salvation of the world, and that He is Christ and also the true Messiah. I beseech you to persevere, promising to you, and all your posterity, to assist you in the presence of My Son."

(Great graces are given to those who carry a copy of this letter.)
Mary Virgin, very humble servant of God

A Prayer for Daily Neglects

Eternal Father, I offer Thee the Sacred Heart of Jesus, with all its love, all its sufferings and all its merits.

First - To expiate all the sins I have committed this day and during all my life.

(Glory be to the Father and to the Son and the Holy Ghost as it was in the beginning, is now, and ever shall be, world without end. Amen.)

Second - To purify the good I have done badly this day and during all my life.

(Glory Be to the Father...)

Third - To minister for the good I ought to have done, and that I have neglected this day and during all my life.

(Glory Be to the Father...)

A poor Clare nun who had just died, appeared to her Abbess, who was praying for her, and said to her, "I went straight to Heaven, for, by means of this prayer, recited every evening, I paid all my debts."

Hail Mary of Gold

Hail Mary, White Lily of the Glorious and always-serene Trinity.
Hail brilliant Rose of the Garden of heavenly delights: O you, by whom God wanted to be born and by whose milk the King of Heaven wanted to be nourished! Nourish our souls with effusions of divine grace. Amen!
At the hour when the soul which has thus greeted me quits the body I will appear to them in such splendid beauty that they'll taste, to their great consolation, something of the joys of Paradise.

The Blessed Virgin to St. Gertrude the Great
(Revelations book III, chapter XVIII)

This picture of Our Lady was drawn by a mystic in Italy. Her hand was guided by Our Lady.

There is a special blessing given each day to the person who carries it and another blessing given each time one looks at it with love.

Good Night to Our Blessed Mother

Night is falling dear Mother; the long day is o'er!
And before thy loved image I am kneeling once more
To thank thee for keeping me safe through the day
To ask thee this night to keep evil away.
Many times, have I fallen today, Mother Dear,
Many graces neglected, since last, I knelt here;
Wilt thou not in pity, my own Mother mild,
Ask Jesus to pardon the sins of thy child?
I am going to rest, for the day's work is done,
Its hours and its moments have passed one by one;
And the God who will judge me has noted them all,
He has numbered each grace, He has counted each fall.
In His book, they are written against the last day,
O Mother, ask Jesus to wash them away;
For one drop of His blood which for sinners was spilt,
Is sufficient to cleanse the whole world of its guilt.
And if ever the dawn I should draw my last breath
And the sleep that I take be the long sleep of death,
Be near me, dear Mother, for dear Jesus' sake
When my soul on Eternity's shore shall awake.

4. Three Very Beautiful Prayers

Which are very useful to a dying person, and should be prayed often as an act of mercy.

There once was a Pope in Rome who was surrounded by many sins. The Lord God struck him with a fatal illness. When he saw that he was dying, he summoned Cardinals, Bishops and learned persons and said to them: "My dear friends! What comfort can you give me now that I must die, and when I deserve eternal damnation for my sins?" No one answered him. One of them, a pious curate named John, said: "Father, why do you doubt the Mercy of God?" The Pope replied: "What comfort can you give me now that I must die and fear that I'll be damned for my sins?" John replied: "I'll read these prayers over you; I hope you'll be comforted and that you will obtain Mercy from God." The Pope was unable to say more. The curate and all those present knelt and said an Our Father, then the following Prayers:

Prayer:1

Lord Jesus Christ! Thou Son of God and Son of the Virgin Mary, God and Man, thou who in fear sweated blood for us on the Mount of Olives in order to bring peace, and to offer Thy Most Holy Death to God Thy Heavenly Father for the salvation of this dying person... If it be, however, that by his sins, he merits eternal damnation, then may it be deflected from him. This, O Eternal Father through Our Lord Jesus Christ, Thy Dear Son, Who liveth and reigneth in union with The Holy Spirit now and forever. Amen

Prayer:2

Lord Jesus Christ! Thou Who meekly died on the trunk of the Cross for us, submitting Thy Will completely to Thy Heavenly Father in order to bring peace and to offer Thy Most Holy Death to Thy Heavenly Father in order to free... (this person) ...and to hide from him what he has earned with his sins; grant this O Eternal Father! Through Our Lord Jesus Thy Son, Who liveth and reigneth with Thee in union with the Holy Spirit now and forever. Amen.

Prayer:3

Lord Jesus Christ! Thou Who remained silent to speak through the mouths of the Prophets: I have drawn Thee to me through Eternal Love, which Love drew Thee from Heaven into the body of the Virgin, which Love drew Thee from the body of the Virgin into the valley of this needful world, which Love kept Thee 33 years in this world, and as a sign of Great Love, Thou hast given Thy Holy Body as True Food and Thy Holy Blood as True Drink, as a sign of Great Love, Thou hast consented to be condemned to death, and hast consented to die and to be buried and truly risen, and appeared to Thy Holy Mother and all Thy Apostles and the hearts of all who hope and believe in Thee. Through Thy Sign of Eternal Love, open Heaven today and take this dying person.... And all his sins into the Realm of Thy Heavenly Father, that he may reign with Thee now and forever. Amen.

Meanwhile, the pope died. The curate persevered to the third hour, then the Pope appeared to him in body and comforting him; his countenance as brilliant as the sun, his clothes as white as snow, and he said: "My dear brother! Whereas I was supposed to be a child of damnation I've become a child of happiness. As you recited the first Prayer, many of my sins fell from me as rain from Heaven, and as you recited the second Prayer, I was purified, as a goldsmith purifies gold in a hot fire. I was still purified as you recited the third Prayer. Then I saw Heaven open and the Lord Jesus standing on the Right Hand of God the Father, who said to me: "Come, all thy sins are forgiven thee, you'll be and remain in the Realm of My Father forever. Amen!"

With these words, my soul separated from my body and the Angels of God led it to Eternal Joy.

As the curate heard this he said: "O Holy Father! I can't tell these things to anyone, for they won't believe me." Then the Pope said: "Truly I tell thee; the Angel of God stands with me and has written the prayers in letters of gold for the consolement of all sinners. If a person had committed all the sins in the world, but that the three Prayers shall have been read (over him) at his end (death), all his sins will be forgiven him, even though his soul was supposed to suffer until the Last Judgement, it will be redeemed (freed)."

The person who hears them read, he won't die an unhappy death, also in whose house they shall be read. Therefore, take these prayers and carry them into St. Peter's Basilica and lay them in the Chapel named the Assumption of Mary, for certain consolation. The person who will be near death, who reads them or hears them read, gains 400 years indulgence for the days he was supposed to suffer in Purgatory because of his guilt. Also, who reads this Prayer or hears it read, the hour of his death shall be revealed to him. Amen!

An Act of Contrition

O my God, I am heartily sorry for all my sins because of them I deserve the eternal pains of hell, but most of all because I have offended Thee my God who art all good and deserving of all my love. I firmly resolve with the help of Thy grace to confess my sins, to do penance, to avoid the proximate occasion of sin and never to sin anymore. Amen.

Tips on Prayer

Your prayers are strongest at the Consecration in Holy Mass (raising of Host and Chalice).

Each time we look at The Most Blessed Sacrament our place in Heaven is raised forever (revealed by Our Lord to St. Gertrude the Great).

Prayer to Obtain the Grace of all the World's Masses

Eternal Father we humbly offer Thee our poor presence and that of the whole of humanity from the beginning to the end of the world at all the Masses that ever have or ever will be prayed. We offer Thee all the pains, suffering, prayers, sacrifices, joys and relaxations of our lives, in union with those of our dear Lord Jesus here on earth. May the Most Precious Blood of Christ, all His blood and wounds and agony save us, through the sorrowful and Immaculate Heart of Mary. Amen!

(This prayer should be prayed daily, and made known.)

Dear St. Philomena, pray for us that purity of mind and heart which lead to the Perfect Love of God!

God Must be pursued and the more you chase him, the more you catch him (Maimonedes)

Graces Derived from Assisting at Mass

1. The Mass is Calvary continued.
2. Every Mass is worth as much as the sacrifice of Our Lord's life, sufferings and death.
3. Holy Mass is the most powerful atonement for your sins.
4. At the hour of death, the Masses you have heard will be your greatest consolement.
5. Every Mass will go with you to judgement and plead for pardon.
6. At Mass, you can diminish more or less temporal punishment due to your sins, according to your fervor.
7. Assisting devoutly at Holy Mass you render to the humanity of Our

Lord the greatest homage.

8. He supplies for many of your negligence's and omissions.
9. He forgives the venial sins which you have not confessed. The power of Satan over you is diminished.
10. You afford the souls in Purgatory the greatest possible relief.
11. One Mass heard during life will be of more benefit to you than many heard for you after your death.
12. You are preserved from dangers and misfortunes which otherwise might have befallen you. You shorten your Purgatory.
13. Every Mass wins you a higher degree of glory in Heaven.
14. You receive the Priest's blessing which Our Lord ratifies in Heaven.
15. You kneel amidst a multitude of Holy Angels, who are present at the adorable Sacrifice with reverential awe.
16. You are blessed in your temporal goods and affairs.

In eternity, we shall fully realize that it was certainly worthwhile to have assisted at Holy Mass daily. **Pray for Priests That They May Offer the Mass with Holy Love and Reverence.**

St. Bonaventure said: "that whoever neglected Our Lady would perish in his sins and would be damned".

Holy Communion

Each time we receive Holy Communion our venial sins are forgotten.

Christ revealed to St. Gertrude the Great that each time one person receives Holy Communion, something good happens to every being in Heaven, on earth, and in Purgatory.

The Cure of Ars said that a Communion well received is worth more than 20,000 NFF given to the poor.

Each time we receive Communion our place in Heaven is raised forever, our stay in Purgatory shortened.

We Should Never Let a Day Pass Without Going to Holy Communion!

Spiritual Communion

The value of a spiritual Communion well-made is enormous. We can, and should, make one frequently. Simply think on Jesus and how much He loves us and how much we love Him, then ask Our Blessed Mother to ask Her Divine Son to come into our hearts. We can offer these Communions for the interest of the Sorrowful and Immaculate Heart of Mary, noting our special intention!

After receiving Holy Communion, Our Lord said we should pray: "Most Sacred Heart of Jesus, may the whole world burn with love for You!" **(revelation to Gabrielle Bosse in France)**.

A True Letter of Our Savior Jesus Christ

Consecrating the Drops of Blood Which Our Lord Jesus lost on His way to Calvary.

Copy of a letter of the Oration found in the Holy Sepulcher of Our Lord Jesus Christ in Jerusalem, preserved in a silver box by His Holiness and by the Emperors and Empresses of the Christian Faith.

St. Elizabeth, Queen of Hungary, with St. Matilda and St. Bridget, wishing to know something of the Passion of Jesus Christ, offered fervent and special prayers, upon which there appeared to them Our Lord Jesus Christ who spoke to them in the following manner:

I descended from Heaven to the Earth in order to convert you.
In olden times, people were religious, and their harvests were abundant; at present, on the contrary, they are scanty.

If you want to reap an abundant harvest you must not work on Sunday, for Sunday you must go to Church and pray to God to forgive your sins. He gave you six days in which to work and one for rest and devotion and to tender your help to the poor and assist the Church.

Those people who brawl against My Religion and cast slurs on this Sacred Letter will be forsaken by Me.

On the contrary, those people who shall carry a copy of this letter with them shall be free from death by drowning and from sudden death. They shall be free from all contagious diseases and lightning; they shall not die without confession, and shall be free from their enemies and from the hand of wrongful authority, and from all their slanderers and false witnesses.

Women in peril at child-birth will, by keeping this Oration about them, immediately overcome the difficulty. In the houses where this Oration is kept, no evil thing will ever happen: and forty days before the death of a person who has this Oration about him or her, the Blessed Virgin will appear to him or her. So, said St. Gregorious.

To all those faithful who shall recite for three years, each day, 2 Our Fathers, Hail Marys, and Glory Be's, in honor of the drops of blood I lost, I will concede the following five graces:.

1st The plenary indulgence and remission of your sins.

2nd You will be free from the pains of Purgatory.

3rd If you should die before completing the said 3 years, for you it will be the same as if you had completed them.

4th It will be upon your death the same as if you had shed all your blood for the Holy Faith.

5th I will descend from Heaven to take your soul and that of your relatives, until the fourth generation.

Be it known that the number of armed soldiers were 150; those who trailed me while I was bound were 23. The number of executioners of justice were 83; the blows received on my head were 150; those on my stomach, 108; kicks on my shoulders, 80. I was led, bound with cords by the hair, 24 times; spits in the face were 180; I was beaten on the body 6666 times; beaten on the head, 110 times. I was roughly pushed, and at 12 o'clock was lifted up by the hair; pricked with thorns and pulled by the beard 23 times; received 20 wounds on the head; thorns of marine junks, 72; pricks of thorns in the head, 110; mortal thorns in the forehead, 3. I was afterwards flogged and dressed as a mocked king; wounds in the body, 1000. The soldiers who led me to the Calvary were 608; those who watched me were 3, and those who mocked me were 1008; the drops of blood which I lost were 28,430.

5. Prayer to The Infant of Prague

O merciful Infant Jesus! I know of Thy miraculous deeds for the sick ... in view of the innumerable graces and the cures granted ... through the veneration of Thy Holy Infancy, particularly in the statue of Prague ... I exclaim with the greatest assurance: O most loving ... Infant Jesus, thou canst cure me if Thou wilt!
Extend Thy Holy Hand and by Thy Power take away all pain and infirmity.

History of The Devotion to The Infant of Prague

Devotion to the Infant Jesus is as old as Christianity itself. It ever tends to keep the great mystery of Our Lord's birth vividly before us.

A special devotion to the Divine Child originated with the Carmelites in the City of Prague, Bohemia, in the beginning of the seventeenth century. Princes Polyxedia of Liebowitz had received, as a wedding gift from her mother, a statue of the Divine Child, previously brought from Spain. After the death of her husband, the princes devoted herself to works of charity and was particularly helpful to the Carmelites in Prague. When in 1628 the Carmelite Monastery had been reduced to poverty, owing to the ravages of war, the princes gave her precious statue to the Carmelites, saying:

"I GIVE YOU WHAT I PRIZE MOST HIGHLY IN THE WORLD; HONOR AND RESPECT THE CHILD JESUS AND YOU SHALL NEVER BE IN WANT."

Her gift was placed in the Carmelite oratory. The words of the princess proved prophetic for as long as the Carmelites kept up their devotion to the Divine Infant of Prague everything prospered with them. The Carmelites were later forced to flee form the city and in the confusion of the war, they were unable to take with them their miraculous statue. The invaders seized it, and threw it into a pile of rubbish. In 1635, peace came to Prague and the Carmelites returned. One of them, Father Cyril, who had previously received great spiritual help through his devotion to the Infant of Prague, sought the statue, and found it amidst the rubbish. Overjoyed, he placed the statue again in the oratory. As Father Cyril was one day praying devotedly before the statue, he heard a voice saying:
"HAVE MERCY ON ME AND I WILL HAVE MERCY ON YOU. RETURN MY HANDS TO ME AND I SHALL GIVE YOU PEACE. THE MORE YOU HONOR ME, THE MORE I SHALL BLESS YOU."

Startled by these words, Father Cyril examined the statue and upon drawing aside the mantle covering it, he found that both hands of the statue were broken off. The hands were restored to the statue through the generosity of a client of the Divine Child. Once more, peace and prosperity returned to the Carmelites.

Devotion to the Divine Child had always been practiced by the Carmelites, for through their Mother, Mary, this Divine Child had come to the world. St. Theresa of Jesus practice particular devotion to the Divine Child. St. Therese, the Little Flower, was also a most fervent venerator.

My Daily Offering

O Jesus, through the immaculate heart of Mary, I offer you my prayers, works, joys and sufferings of this day in union with the holy sacrifice of the Mass throughout the world. I offer them for all the intentions of your sacred heart: the salvation of souls, reparation for sin, the reunion of all Christians. I offer them for the intentions of our bishops and of all the apostles of prayer, and in particular for those recommended by our Holy Father this month.

6. Daily Prayer to Guardian Angel

Angel of God
My guardian dear
To Whom His love
Commits me here
Ever this day
Be at my side
To light and guard
To rule and guide. Amen

"Say daily upon arising, 7 Glory Be's to your guardian angel."

6. Prayers After Mass and Communion

Prayer Before a Crucifix

Look down upon me good and gentle Jesus, while before Thy face I humbly kneel and with burning soul pray and beseech Thee to fix deep in my heart lively sentiments of faith, hope and charity, true contrition for my sins and a firm purpose of amendment, while I contemplate with great love and tender pity Thy Five Wounds, pondering over them within me and calling to mind the words which David Thy prophet said of Thee my Jesus, "They have pierced My Hands and My Feet, they have numbered all My Bones." (Ps. 21, 17-18)

Our Father, Hail Mary, Glory Be, for our Holy Father's intentions; Plenary indulgence when said after Communion; (S. Paen, Ap., 2 Feb 1934)

ANIMA CHRISTI

Soul of Christ, sanctify me.
Body of Christ, save me.
Blood of Christ, inebriate me.
Water from the side of Christ, wash me.
Passion of Christ, strengthen me.
O good Jesus, hear me.
Within Thy wounds, hide me.
Suffer me not to be separated from Thee.
From the malignant enemy, defend me.
In the hour of my death, call me.
And bid me come to Thee.
That with Thy saints I may praise Thee.
Forever and ever.   Amen.

An indulgence of 300 days. An indulgence of 7 years, if recited after Holy Communion.
St. Ignatius Loyola

Rosary of the Holy Wounds of Our Lord Jesus Christ or Chaplet of Mercy

May be said on the Rosary Beads.

On the large beads:
Eternal Father, I offer Thee the WOUNDS of Our Lord Jesus Christ -- To heal the wounds of our souls.
(300 days indulgence each time)

On the small beads:
My Jesus, pardon and mercy -- Through the merits of Thy HOLY WOUNDS.
(300 days indulgence each time)
Sacred Penetentiary, January 15, 1924.

These two invocations were taught by Our Lord to Sr. M. Martha

Chambon, deceased, in the Visitation of Chambery, France, March 21, 1907. The Sister received from Our Lord a double "Mission": constantly to invoke the HOLY WOUNDS herself, and to revive this devotion in the world.

Promises of Our Lord to Sr. Mary Martha

"I will grant all that is asked of me by the invocation of My HOLY WOUNDS. You must spread the devotion."

Prayer to Defeat the Work of Satan

O Divine Eternal Father, in union with your Divine Son and the Holy Spirit, and through the Immaculate Heart of Mary, I beg You to destroy the power of your greatest enemy -- the evil spirits.

Cast them in to the deepest recesses of hell and chain them there forever! Take possession of your Kingdom, which You have created and which is rightfully yours.

Heavenly Father, give us the reign of the Sacred Heart of Jesus and the Immaculate Heart of Mary.

I repeat this prayer out of pure love for You with every beat of my heart and with every breath that I take. Amen.

Imprimatur, March 1973, +Richard H. Ackerman
Bishop of Covington

C.H.G.   J.M.J.

TAKE TIME TO PRAY . . ..
It is the greatest power on earth!
WHEN YOU PRAY . . ..
"Say what you mean, and mean what you say."

"Pray without ceasing"

28

THE JESUS PRAYER

Lord Jesus Christ, have mercy on me" (say 600 times a day)

"GOD GOVERNS THE WORLD
BUT PRAYER GOVERNS GOD"

In the name of the Father and of the Son and of the Holy Spirit. Amen.
Come Holy Ghost, fill the hearts of Thy faithful and enkindle in them the fire of Thy love.
V. Send forth Thy Spirit and They shall be created.
 R. And Thou shalt renew the face of the earth.
Let us pray
O God, who by the light of the Holy Spirit, didst instruct the hearts of the faithful, grant that in the same Spirit we may be truly wise and ever rejoice in His consolation, through Christ Our Lord. Amen.
Indulgence of five years. Plenary indulgences, under the usual conditions, if the prayer has been recited daily far a month.
Enchiridion lndulgentium, 287

SAY DAILY UPON ARISING:

7 "Glory Be's to the Holy Ghost"

CHAPLET OF FAITH
On each decade of the rosary pray;
on large bead: One Apostles Creed -
on 10 small beads: Jesus, Mary, I love you, save souls,
save the consecrated -
at the end, 5 times; Hail Holy Queen.

Blessed Virgin Mary to Saint Dominic, "One Day through the Rosary and Scapular I will save the World"

"Whosoever dies clothed in this (scapular) shall not suffer eternal fire.
This is Mary's Promise made July 16, 1261 to Saint Simon Stock.

The devils revealed to Francis of Yepes, the brother of St. John of the Cross, that three things especially tormented them. The first is the Name of Jesus; the second, the Name of Mary, and the third, the Brown Scapular of Our Lady of Mt. Carmel. "Take off that habit," they cried to him, "which snatches so many souls from us. All those clothed in it die piously and escape us."

Your SCAPULAR, then should take on deep meaning for you. It is a rich present brought down from Heaven by
OUR LADY HERSELF
"Wear it devoutly and perseveringly," she says to each soul, "it is my garment. To be clothed in it means you are continually thinking of me, and I in turn, am always thinking of you and helping you to secure eternal life."

Prayer of St. Simon Stock
Known as the FLOS CARMELI, the following prayer has for seven centuries been called a prayer to the Blessed Mother which has *never been known to fail* in obtaining her powerful help.

Prayer

O beautiful Flower of Carmel, most fruitful vine, Splendor of Heaven, holy and singular, who brought forth the Son of God, still ever remaining a Pure Virgin, assist me in this necessity. O Star of the Sea, help and protect me! Show me that Thou art my Mother.

O Mary, conceived without sin,
Pray for us who have recourse to thee!

Mother and Ornament of Carmel, Pray for us!
Virgin. Flower of Carmel, pray for us!
Patroness of all who wear the Scapular, pray for us!
Hope of all who die wearing the Scapular, pray for us!
St. Joseph, Friend of the Sacred Heart, pray for us!
St. Joseph, Chaste Spouse of Mary, pray for us!
St. Joseph, Our Patron, pray for us!
O sweet Heart of Mary, Be our Salvation.

The Fifteen Promises of Mary
to Christians Who Recite the Rosary

1. Whoever shall faithfully serve me by the recitation of the rosary, shall receive signal graces.
2. I promise my special protection and the greatest graces to all those who shall recite the rosary.
3. The rosary shall be a powerful armor against hell, it will destroy vice, decrease sin, and defeat heresies.
4. It will cause virtue and good works to flourish; it will obtain for souls the abundant mercy of God; it will withdraw the hearts of men from the love of the world and its vanities, and will lift them to the desire of eternal things. Oh, that souls would sanctify themselves by this means.
5. The soul which recommends itself to me by the recitation of the rosary, shall not perish.
6. Whoever shall recite the rosary devoutly, applying himself to the consideration of its sacred mysteries shall never be conquered by misfortune. God will not chastise him in His justice, he shall not perish by an unprovided death; if he be just he shall remain in the grace of God, and become worthy of eternal life
7. Whoever shall have a true devotion for the rosary shall not die without the sacraments of the Church.
8. Those who are faithful to recite the rosary shall have during their life and at their death the light of God and the plentitude of His graces; at the moment of death they shall participate in the merits

of the saints in paradise.

9. I shall deliver from purgatory those who have been devoted to the rosary.

10. The faithful children of the rosary shall merit a high degree of glory in heaven.

11. You shall obtain all you ask of me by the recitation of the rosary.

12. All those who propagate the holy rosary shall be aided by me in their necessities.

13. I have obtained from my Divine Son that all the advocates of the rosary shall have for intercessors the entire celestial court during their life and at the hour of death.

14. All who recite the rosary are my sons, and brothers of my only son Jesus Christ.

15. Devotion of my rosary is a great sign of predestination.

(Given to St. Dominic and Blessed Alan) Imprimatur:
+PATRICK J. HAYES. D.D.. Archbishop of New York

WHY the daily rosary?

Our Lady has 117 titles. She selected this title at Fatima:
"I am the Lady of the Rosary".
St. Francis de Sales said the greatest method of praying
IS - Pray the Rosary.
St. Thomas Aquinas preached 40 straight days in Rome,
Italy on just the Hail Mary.

St. John Vianney, patron of priests, was seldom seen without a rosary in his hand.

"The rosary is the scourge of the devil" - Pope Adrian VI.

"The rosary is a treasure of graces" - Pope Paul V.

Padre Pio the stigmatic priest said: "The rosary is **THE WEAPON**"

Pope Leo XIII wrote 9 encyclicals on the rosary.

Pope John XXIII spoke 38 times about our Lady and the Rosary. He prayed 15 decades daily.

St. Louis Marie Grignion de Montfort wrote:
"The rosary is the most powerful weapon to touch the
Heart of Jesus, Our Redeemer, who so loves His Mother."

If you wish to obtain a favor: -
Pray THE "54-day ROSARY NOVENA"...
Pray 3 nine-day rosary novenas - 27 days of petition;
Pray 3 nine-day rosary novenas - 27 days of thanksgiving.
Will you give 1% of 1440 minutes each day to God?
If so, pray the daily rosary in 15 minutes - 1% of 24 hours.
Later, give 3% and pray entire 15-decade rosary.
Joyful, Sorrowful and Glorious Mysteries.

"Why Should I Go to Mass Every Day?"

"The Mass is the most perfect form of prayer!"
(Pope Paul VI)
For each Mass we hear with devotion, Our Lord sends a saint to comfort us at death (revelation of Christ to St. Gertrude the great).

Padre Pio, the stigmatic priest, said, the world could exist more easily without the sun than without the Mass.
The Cure' d' Ars, St. Jean Vianney said, if we knew the value of the Mass we would die of joy.

A great doctor of the Church, St. Anselm, declares that a single Mass offered for oneself during life may be worth more than a thousand celebrated for the same intention after death. St. Leonard of Port Maurice supports this statement by saying that one Mass before death may be more profitable than many after it.

"The Holy Mass would be of greater profit if people had it offered in their lifetime, rather than having it celebrated for the relief of their souls after death."
(Pope Benedict XV).

Once, St. Teresa was overwhelmed with God's Goodness and asked Our Lord, "How can I thank you?" Our Lord replied, "ATTEND ONE MASS."

The Blessed Virgin Mary once told Her faithful servant Alain: "My Son so loves those who assist at the Holy Sacrifice of the Mass that, if it were necessary He would die for them as many times as they've heard Masses." (Page 107, last paragraph of "Explication Du Saint Sacrifice De La Messe" parle R.P. Martin de Cochem Friere - Mineur Capucin.)

"Jesus, Mary, I Love You, Save Souls"

7. A Short Way of The Cross

As used by the Franciscan Fathers on their Missions

First Station
Jesus Condemned to Death
O Jesus! so meek and uncomplaining, teach me resignation in trials.

Second Station
Jesus Carries His Cross
My Jesus, this Cross should be mine, not Thine; my sins crucified Thee.

Third Station
Our Lord Falls the First Time
O Jesus! by this first fall, never let me fall into mortal sin.

Fourth Station
Jesus Meets His Mother
O Jesus! may no human tie, however dear, keep me from following the road of the Cross.

Fifth Station
Simon the Cyrenean Helps Jesus Carry His Cross
Simon unwillingly assisted Thee; may I with patience suffer all for Thee.

Sixth Station
Veronica Wipes the Face of Jesus
O Jesus! Thou didst imprint Thy sacred features upon Veronica's veil; stamp them also indelibly upon my heart.

Seventh Station
The Second Fall of Jesus
By Thy second fall, preserve me, dear Lord, from relapse into sin.

Eighth Station
Jesus Consoles the Women of Jerusalem

My greatest consolation would be to hear Thee say: "Many sins are forgiven thee, because thou hast loved much."

Ninth Station
Third Fall of Jesus

O Jesus! when weary upon life's long journey, be Thou my strength and my perseverance.

Tenth Station
Jesus Stripped of His Garments

My soul has been robbed of its robe of innocence; clothe me, dear Jesus, with the garb of penance and contrition.

Eleventh Station
Jesus Nailed to the Cross

Thou didst forgive Thy enemies; my God, teach me to forgive injuries and FORGET them.

Twelfth Station
Jesus Dies on the Cross

Thou art dying, my Jesus, but Thy Sacred Heart still throbs with love for Thy sinful children.

Thirteenth Station
Jesus Taken Down from the Cross

Receive me into thy arms, O Sorrowful Mother; and obtain for me perfect contrition for my sins.

Fourteenth Station
Jesus Laid in the Sepulcher

When I receive Thee into my heart in Holy Communion, O Jesus, make it a fit abiding place for Thy Adorable Body. Amen.

The 4 keys to heaven
MASS
ROSARY
SCAPULAR
WAY OF THE CROSS

"Jesus, Mary, I love You, Save Souls"

BROTHER ESTANISLAO (1903 - 1927)

At the age of 18, a young Spaniard entered the Novitiate of The Brothers of the Christian Schools at Bugedo. He took the Vow of Regularity, Perfection and Pure Love. In October, 1926, he offered himself to Jesus through Mary. Soon after this heroic donation, he felt ill, and was obliged to rest. He died saintly in March 1927. He was, according to the master of novices, a privileged soul, who received Messages from Heaven. Confessors and Theologians recognized these supernatural facts. His Director asked him to write the Promises made by OUR LORD to those who have devotion to THE WAY OF THE CROSS: They are:

1. I will grant everything that is asked of Me with faith, when making The Way of the Cross.
2. I promise Eternal Life to those who pray from time to time, The Way of the Cross.
3. I will follow them everywhere in life and I will help them, especially at the hour of death.
4. Even if they have more sins than the blades of grass in the fields and the grains of sand in the sea, all of them will be erased by The Way of the Cross. (Note: This promise does not eliminate the obligation to confess all mortal sins, and this, before we can receive Holy Communion.)
5. Those who pray The Way of the Cross often will have a special glory in Heaven.
6. I will deliver them from Purgatory, indeed if they go there at all, the first Tuesday or Friday after their death.
7. I will bless them at each Way of the Cross, and My blessing will follow them everywhere on earth and, after their death, in Heaven for all Eternity.
8. At the hour of death I will not permit the devil to tempt them; I will lift all power from him in order that they will repose tranquilly in My Arms.
9. If they pray it with true love, I will make of each one of them a living Ciborium in which it will please Me to pour My grace.
10. I will fix My Eyes on those who pray The Way of the Cross often; My hands will always be open to protect them.
11. As I am nailed to the Cross, so also will I always be with those who honor Me in making The Way of the Cross frequently.
12. They will never be able to separate themselves from Me, for I will give them the grace never again to commit a Mortal sin.
13. At the hour of death I will console them with My Presence and we will go together to Heaven. Death will be sweet to all those who have honored

Me during their lives by praying The Way of the Cross.

14. My soul will be a protective shield for them, and will always help them, whenever they have recourse.

"Jesus, Mary, I love You, Save Souls"

St. Alphonsus Liguori wrote: **"If you pray you are positive of saving your soul. If you do NOT pray you are just as positive of losing your soul."**

Prayer to the Shoulder Wound of Jesus

O Loving Jesus, meek Lamb of God, I a miserable sinner, salute and worship the most Sacred Wound of Thy Shoulder on which Thou didst bear Thy Heavy Cross, which so tore Thy Flesh and laid bare Thy Bones as to inflict on Thee an anguish greater than any other Wound of Thy Most Blessed Body. I adore Thee, O Jesus most sorrowful; I praise and glorify Thee and give Thee thanks for this most sacred and painful Wound, beseeching Thee by that exceeding pain and by the crushing burden of Thy Heavy Cross to be merciful to me, a sinner, to forgive me all my mortal and venial sins, and to lead me on towards Heaven along the Way of Thy Cross. Amen.

Imprimatur: Thomas D. Beven, Bishop of Springfield, Ma.

It is related in the annals of Clairvaux that St. Bernard asked Our Lord which was His greatest unrecorded suffering and Our Lord answered: "I had on My Shoulder, while I bore My Cross on the Way of Sorrows, a grievous Wound, which was more painful than the others and which is not recorded by men. Honor this Wound with thy devotion and I will grant thee whatsoever thou dost ask through Its virtue and merit. And in regard to all those who shall venerate this Wound, I will remit to them all their venial sins and will no longer remember their mortal sins."

8. Invocations in Honor Of
The Holy Wounds of Our Lord Jesus Christ

Eternal Father I offer Thee the Wounds of Our Lord Jesus Christ to heal the wounds of our souls. My Jesus, pardon and mercy through the merits of Thy Sacred Wounds.

Sister Mary Martha Chambon, a humble lay Sister of the Visitation Order of Chambery. France, who died in the odor of sanctity, March 21st, 1907, received these two invocations from Our Lord Himself, as she affirmed, and with them a double MISSION to adore and invoke the Sacred Wounds unceasingly and to revive this devotion in the hearts of creatures.

Our Lord said:
"The soul who during life has honored and studied the Wounds of Our Lord Jesus Christ, and has offered them to the Eternal Father for the souls in Purgatory, will be accompanied at the moment of death by the Holy Virgin and the angels; and Our Lord on the Cross all brilliant in glory will receive her and crown her."

"Jesus, Mary, I love You, Save Souls."

Pray for Souls in Purgatory

There are more souls released from purgatory during the Consecration of the Mass than at any time. Christmas is the day of the year when most souls are delivered; then feast days of Our Lord, Our Lady and great saints. Souls receive much grace from prayers offered for them on their birthdays, day of baptism, anniversary of death.

The more we work for Poor Souls on earth the more others will pray for us, the more merciful will Christ be with us when were in purgatory.

Our Lady asked that we pray very much for the poor souls; that we pray:

5   I believe in God . . .

1   Hail Holy Queen . . .

1   Our Father . . .

1   Hail Mary . . .

1   Glory be to the Father . . .

1   Requiem (Eternal rest grant unto them O Lord and let perpetual light shine upon them and may they rest in peace. Amen!)

PRAYER OF ST. GERTRUDE THE GREAT

A Prayer which would release 1,000 souls from Purgatory each time it is said.

Our Lord told St. Gertrude the GREAT that the following prayer would release 1,000 souls from Purgatory each time it is said.

Recommendations: Pray it at least twice, to at least release twice as many souls! After the prayer, ask the Holy Souls to pray for your intentions.

"Eternal Father, I offer thee the most precious blood of thy Divine Son, Jesus, in union with the Masses said throughout the world today, for all the Holy Souls in Purgatory. -Amen"

Our Lady said that if we pray the prayers "we'll deliver so many souls, so many souls!"

"The Holy wounds are the treasure of treasures for the souls in Purgatory."

BIBLE - 2 Machabees, Chapter 12. Verse 46:

"it is therefore a holy and wholesome thought to pray for the dead, that they may be loosed from sins."

An indulgence, applicable ONLY to the Souls in Purgatory, is granted when the faithful devoutly visit a cemetery and pray for the departed.

The Spiritual Communion

By a rescript of November 24. 1922 the Sacred Congregation of Indulgences approved the following formula for a spiritual communion:

"O Jesus I turn toward the holy tabernacle where You live hidden for love of me. I love you, O my God. I cannot receive you in Holy Communion. Come nevertheless and visit me with Your grace. Come spiritually into my heart. Purify it. Sanctify it. Render it like unto Your own. Amen.
Lord, I am not worthy that thou should enter under my roof, but only say the word and my soul shall be healed.

An indulgence of 500 days, if thrice repeated. (129 The Raccolta 1944).
It was the Cure of Ars who said, "A spiritual communion acts on the soul as blowing does on a cinder-covered fire which was about to go out. Whenever you feel your love of God growing cold, quickly make a spiritual communion."

Message of World-Wide Importance
Devotion to the Sorrowful and Immaculate Heart of Mary

This Message was confided by Our Lord to Berthe Petit, a humble Franciscan Tertiary, born on January 23, 1870, at Enghien, Belgium:
"Teach souls to love the Heart of My Mother pierced by the very sorrows which pierced Mine." (December 25, 1909)
At the Holy Hour (March 25, 1912) the Blessed Virgin spoke thus: "I have called myself the Immaculate Conception. To you I call myself Mother of the Sorrowful Heart. This title willed by my Son is dear to me above all others. According as it is spread everywhere, there will be granted graces of mercy, spiritual renewal and salvation."

PRAYER (Composed by Berthe Petit)
Sorrowful and Immaculate Heart of Mary, dwelling pure and holy, cover my soul with your maternal protection so that being ever faithful to the voice of Jesus, it responds to His love and obeys His Divine Will.
I wish, O, my Mother, to keep unceasingly before me your co-redemption in order to live intimately with your Heart that is totally united to the Heart of your Divine Son.
Fasten me to this Heart by your own virtues and sorrows.
Protect me always.

9. The Prayer or Blessing Against Storms

is of great importance (At each '✝', make the Sign of The Cross)

Jesus Christ a King of Glory has come in Peace. ✝
God became man, ✝
and the Word was made flesh. ✝
Christ was born of a Virgin. ✝
Christ suffered. ✝
Christ was crucified. ✝
Christ died. ✝
Christ rose from the dead. ✝
Christ ascended into Heaven. ✝
Christ conquers. ✝
Christ reigns. ✝
Christ orders. ✝
May Christ protect us from all storms and lightning✝
Christ went through their midst in Peace, ✝
and the word was made flesh. ✝
Christ is with us with Mary. ✝
Flee you enemy spirits because the Lion of the Generation of Juda,
the Root David, has won. ✝
Holy God! ✝
Holy Powerful God! ✝
Holy Immortal God! ✝
Have mercy on us.
Amen!

Above, in Millet's famous painting, a peasant boy and girl in France
recite the Angelus at dark.
"The Angel of the Lord declared unto Mary..."
It is one of the most famous paintings in the world.

6—12—6

The Angelus

V.   The Angel of the Lord declared unto Mary.

R. And she conceived of the Holy Ghost. *("Hail Mary"*
Prayer)

V.   Behold the handmaid of the Lord.

R.   Be it done unto me according to thy word. *("Hail*
Mary" Prayer)

V.   And the word was made flesh.

R.   And dwelt among us. *("Hail Mary)*

V.   Pray for us, O holy Mother of God.

R.   That we may be made worthy of the promises of
Christ

Let us pray: Pour forth, we beseech Thee, O Lord, thy grace into our
hearts, that we to whom the Incarnation of Christ, Thy Son, was
made known by the message of an angel, may by His Passion and
Cross be brought to the glory of His resurrection, through the same
Christ Our Lord. Amen.
"Jesus, Mary, I love You, Save Souls."

PRAYER TO ST. MICHAEL

St. Michael the Archangel, defend us in the day of Battle; Be our safeguard against the wickedness and snares of the Devil. May God rebuke him, we humbly pray, and do Thou, O Prince of the Heavenly Host, by the power of God, cast into Hell, Satan and all the other evil spirits, who prowl through the world, seeking the ruin of souls.
Amen

This powerful prayer of exorcism was composed by Pope Leo XIII; in a vision, he had been shown the fearful battle to be waged between Satan and St. Michael, over the Church of the future. Now, as never before, the Church needs the intercession of St. Michael Please say this prayer every day.)

MARY, QUEEN OF THE HOLY ANGELS -- PRAY FOR US!
"Jesus, Mary, I love You, Save Souls."

Sincere Act of Contrition

CHAPLET of ST. MICHAEL

Saint Michael appearing one day to Antonia d' Astonac, a most devout Servant of God, told her that he wished to be honored by nine salutations corresponding to the nine Choirs of Angels, which should consist of one Our Father and three Hail Mary's in honor of each of the angelic choirs.

Promises of St. Michael

Whosoever would practice this devotion in his honor would have, when approaching the Holy Table, an escort of nine angels chosen from each one of the nine choirs. In addition, for the daily recital of these nine salutations he promised his continual assistance and that of all the holy angels during life, and after death deliverance from purgatory for themselves and their relations.

Method of Reciting the Chaplet

The chaplet is begun by saying the following invocation on the
medal:
O God, come to my assistance.
O Lord, make haste to help me.
Glory be to the Father, etc.

Following the arrow on the diagram 1-9, say one Our Father and
three Hail Mary's after each of the following nine salutations in honor
of the nine choirs of angels.
1. By the intercession of St. Michael and the celestial Choir of
Seraphim, may the Lord make us worthy to burn with the fire of
perfect charity. Amen.
2. By the intercession of St. Michael and the celestial Choir of
Cherubim, may the Lord vouchsafe to grant us grace to leave the
ways of wickedness to run in the paths of Christian perfection.
Amen.

3. By the intercession of St. Michael and the celestial Choir of
Thrones, may the Lord infuse into our hearts a true and sincere spirit
of humility. Amen.
4. By the intercession of St. Michael and the celestial Choir of
Dominions, may the Lord give us grace to govern our senses and
subdue our unruly passions. Amen.

5. By the intercession of St. Michael and the celestial Choir of Powers, may the Lord vouchsafe to protect our souls against the snares and temptations of the devil. Amen.

6. By the intercession of St. Michael and the celestial Choir of Virtues may the Lord preserve us from evil and suffer us not to fall into temptation. Amen.

7. By the intercession of St. Michael and the celestial Choir of Principalities, may God fill our souls with a true spirit of obedience. Amen.

8. By the intercession of St. Michael and the celestial Choir of Archangels, may the Lord give us perseverance in faith and in all good works, in order that we gain the glory of Paradise. Amen.

9. By the intercession of St. Michael and the celestial Choir of Angels, may the Lord grant us to be protected by them in this mortal life and conducted hereafter to eternal glory. Amen.
Following the arrow on the diagram, 10-13, say one Our Father in honor of each of the following leading angels:
10 St. Michael;
11 St. Gabriel;
12 St. Raphael;
13 our Guardian Angel.

The chaplet is concluded with the following prayers:
O glorious Prince St. Michael, chief and commander of the heavenly hosts, guardian of souls, vanquisher of rebel spirits, servant in the house of the Divine King, and our admirable conductor, thou who dost shine with excellence and superhuman virtue, vouchsafe to deliver us from all evil, who turn to thee with confidence, and enable us by thy gracious protection to serve God more and more faithfully every day.
V. Pray for us, O glorious St. Michael, Prince of the Church of Jesus Christ. R. That we may be made worthy of His promises.

PRAYER

Almighty and Everlasting God, who by a prodigy of goodness and a merciful desire for the salvation of all men, hast appointed the most glorious Archangel, St. Michael, Prince of Thy Church, make us worthy, we beseech Thee, to be delivered from all our enemies that none of them may harass us at the hour of death, but that we may be conducted, by him into the august presence of Thy Divine Majesty. This we beg through the merits of Jesus Christ our Lord. Amen.

(With Ecclesiastical Approval)
SALVE REGINA
Hail, Holy Queen

Hail, Holy Queen, Mother of Mercy, our life, our sweetness and our hope! To thee do we cry, poor banished children of Eve; to thee do we send up our sighs, mourning and weeping in this valley of tears. Turn then, most gracious advocate, thine eyes of mercy towards us; and after this our exile, show unto us the blessed fruit of thy womb, Jesus. O clement, O loving, O Sweet Virgin Mary. Amen. It may be prayed standing - or arms extended - or sung.
"An Indulgence of 5 years"

TWENTY-FOUR "GLORIA BEs TO THE FATHER" NOVENA
to Saint Theresa of the Child Jesus Asking for Necessary Favors

ORIGIN OF THE NOVENA

Father Putigan, a Jesuit, began the Novena to Saint Theresa of the Child Jesus on December 3, 1925, asking the glorious Saint for one great favor. For nine days he recited the "Glory be to the Father" twenty-four times thanking the Holy Trinity for the favors and Graces showered on Saint Theresa during the twenty-four years of her life on earth. The priest asked Saint Theresa, that as a sign that his novena was heard he would receive from someone a freshly plucked rose. On the third day of the novena, an unknown person sought out Father Putigan and presented him with a beautiful rose.

Father Putigan began the second novena on December 24 of the same year, and as a sign, asked for a white rose On the fourth day of this novena one of the Sister-nurses brought him a white rose saying:

"Saint Theresa sent you this."

Amazed, the priest asked: "Where did you get this?"

"I was in the chapel," said the Sister, "and as I was leaving I passed the altar above which hangs the beautiful picture of Saint Theresa.

This rose fell at my feet. I wanted to put it back into the bouquet, but a thought came to me that I should bring it to you."

Father Putigan received the favors he had petitioned of the Little Flower of Jesus, and promised to spread the novena to increase devotion to, and bring her more honor.

In this fashion, from the ninth to the seventeenth of each month, those who want to participate in the Twenty-four "Glory be to the Father's" novena, should add to those of their own, the intentions of all who are at that time making the novena, thus forming one great prayer in common.

THE NOVENA

The Twenty-four "Glory be to the Father's" novena can be said at any time. However, the ninth to the seventeenth or the month is particularly recommended, for on those days the petitioner joins in prayer with all those making the novena.

The "Glory Be to the Father" praising the Holy Trinity is said twenty-four times each of the nine days in thanksgiving for all the blessings and favors given to Saint Theresa or the Child Jesus during the twenty-four years or her life. In addition, this or a similar prayer may be used:

Holy Trinity, God the Father, God the Son, and God the Holy Ghost, I thank Thee for all the blessings and favors Thou hast showered upon the soul of Thy servant Theresa of the Child Jesus, during the twenty-four years she spent here on earth, and in consideration of the merits of this Thy most beloved Saint, I beseech Thee to grant me this favor, if it is in accordance with Thy most Holy Will and is not an obstacle to my salvation."

After this Prayer, follow the twenty-four "Glory be to the Father's" between each of which may be included this short prayer:

"Saint Theresa of the Child Jesus, pray for us.

"The Little Flower"

"I wish to spend my heaven in doing good upon earth."

ST. THERESE, THE LITTLE
FLOWER, PLEASE PICK ME
A ROSE FROM THE HEAVENLY
GARDEN AND SEND IT TO
ME WITH A MESSAGE OF LOVE.
ASK GOD TO GRANT ME THE
FAVOR I THEE IMPLORE AND
TELL HIM I WILL LOVE
HIM EACH DAY MORE AND MORE.

(The above prayer, plus 5 Our Father's, 5 Hail Mary's, 5 Glory Be's, must be said on 5 successive days, before 11 a.m. On the 5th day, the 5th set of prayers having been completed, offer one more set - 5 Our Father's, 5 Hail Mary's, 5 Glory Be's.) TRY IT - IT WORKS

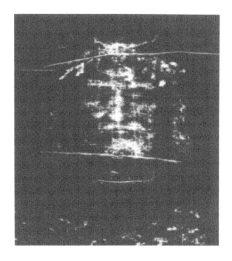

FACE OF JESUS
from the Holy Shroud of Turin

PRAYER
(Composed by St. Therese of Lisieux)

Jesus, Who in Thy Bitter Passion didst become "the reproach of men and
the Man of Sorrows", I venerate Thy Holy Face on which shone the beauty
and gentleness of Divinity. In those disfigured features, I recognize Thine
infinite love, and I long to love Thee and to make Thee loved...
May I behold Thy Glorious Face in Heaven! (St. Therese's name in Religion
was Therese of the Child Jesus and the Holy Face).
Imprimatur: JOANNES HENRICUS Ep. Portus Magni die 3 Oct.
1958.*"Jesus, Mary. I Love You, Save Souls"*

THE GOLDEN ARROW

May the most holy, most sacred, most adorable, most mysterious and
unutterable Name of God be always praised, blessed, loved, adored
and glorified in heaven, on earth and under the earth, by all the
creatures of God, and by the Sacred Heart of our Lord Jesus Christ in
the most Holy Sacrament of the altar.

This prayer was revealed by Our Lard to a Carmelite Nun of Tours in
1843 as a reparation for blasphemy.

"This Golden Arrow will wound My Heart delightfully," He said,
"and heal the wounds inflicted by blasphemy."

10. Chaplet of The Divine Mercy

Jesus I Trust in You!

The Chaplet of Mercy is recited using ordinary rosary beads of five decades. The Chaplet is preceded by two opening prayers from the Diary of Saint Faustina and followed by a closing prayer.

1. Make the Sign of the Cross
In the name of the Father, and of the Son, and of the Holy Spirit. Amen.
2. Optional Opening Prayers
You expired, Jesus, but the source of life gushed forth for souls, and the ocean of mercy opened up for the whole world. O Fount of Life, unfathomable Divine Mercy, envelop the whole world and empty Yourself out upon us.

(Repeat three times)
O Blood and Water, which gushed forth from the Heart of Jesus as a fountain of Mercy for us, I trust in You!
3. Our Father
Our Father, who art in heaven, hallowed be Thy name; Thy kingdom come; Thy will be done on earth as it is in heaven. Give us this day our daily bread; and forgive us our trespasses as we forgive those who trespass against us; and lead us not into temptation, but deliver us from evil, Amen.
4. Hail Mary
Hail Mary, full of grace. The Lord is with thee. Blessed art thou amongst women, and blessed is the fruit of thy womb, Jesus. Holy Mary, Mother of God, pray for us sinners, now and at the hour of our death, Amen.

5. The Apostle's Creed
I believe in God, the Father almighty, Creator of heaven and earth, and in

Jesus Christ, His only Son, our Lord, who was conceived by the Holy Spirit, born of the Virgin Mary, suffered under Pontius Pilate, was crucified, died and was buried; He descended into hell; on the third day He rose again from the dead; He ascended into heaven, and is seated at the right hand of God the Father almighty; from there He will come to judge the living and the dead. I believe in the Holy Spirit, the holy catholic Church, the communion of saints, the forgiveness of sins, the resurrection of the body, and life everlasting. Amen.

6. The Eternal Father

Eternal Father, I offer you the Body and Blood, Soul and Divinity of Your Dearly Beloved Son, Our Lord, Jesus Christ, in atonement for our sins and those of the whole world.

7. On the Ten Small Beads of Each Decade

For the sake of His Sorrowful Passion, have mercy on us and on the whole world.

8. Repeat for the remaining decades

Saying the "Eternal Father" (6) on the "Our Father" bead and then 10 "For the sake of His Sorrowful Passion" (7) on the following "Hail Mary" beads.

9. Conclude with Holy God (Repeat three times)

Holy God, Holy Mighty One, Holy Immortal One, have mercy on us and on the whole world.

10. Optional Closing Prayer

Eternal God, in whom mercy is endless and the treasury of compassion — inexhaustible, look kindly upon us and increase Your mercy in us, that in difficult moments we might not despair nor become despondent, but with great confidence submit ourselves to Your holy will, which is Love and Mercy itself.

Here is your formula of
Consecration to Jesus Christ. The Incarnate Wisdom Through the Blessed Virgin Mary
by St. Louis De Montfort

O Eternal and Incarnate Wisdom! O sweetest and most adorable Jesus! True God and true man, only Son of the Eternal Father, and of Mary, always Virgin! I adore Thee profoundly in the bosom and splendors of Thy Father during eternity; and I adore Thee also in the virginal bosom of Mary, Thy most worthy Mother, in the time of Thine Incarnation.

I give Thee thanks for that Thou hast annihilated Thyself, taking the form of a slave in order to rescue me from the cruel slavery of the devil. I praise and glorify Thee for that Thou hast been pleased to submit Thyself to Mary, thy holy Mother, in all things, in order to make me Thy faithful slave through her. But Alas! Ungrateful and faithless as I have been, I have not kept the promises which I made so solemnly to Thee in my Baptism; I have not fulfilled my obligations; I do not deserve to be called Thy child, nor yet Thy slave; and as there is nothing in me which does not merit Thine anger and Thy repulse, I dare not come by myself before Thy most holy and august majesty. It is on this account that I have recourse to the intercession of Thy most holy Mother, whom Thou hast given me for a mediatrix with Thee. It is through her that I hope to obtain of Thee Contrition, the pardon of my sins, and the acquisition and preservation of wisdom.

Hail, then, O Immaculate Mary, living tabernacle of the Divinity, where the Eternal Wisdom willed to be hidden and to be adored by angels and by men! Hail, O Queen of Heaven and earth, to whose empire everything is subject which is under God. Hail, O sure refuge of sinners, whose mercy fails no one. Hear the desires which I have of the Divine Wisdom; and for that end receive the vows and offerings which in my lowliness I present to thee. I, N., . . .a faithless sinner, renew and ratify today in thy hands the vows of my Baptism; I renounce forever Satan, his pomp's and works; and I give myself entirely to Jesus Christ, the Incarnate Wisdom, to carry my cross after him all the days of my life, and to be more faithful to Him than I have ever been before.

In the presence of all the heavenly court I choose thee this day for my Mother and mistress. I deliver and consecrate to thee, as thy slave, my body and soul, my goods, both interior and exterior, and even the value of all my good actions, past, present and future; leaving to thee the entire and full right of disposing of me, and all that belongs to me, without exception, according to thy good pleasure, for the greater glory of God in time and in eternity.

Receive, O benignant Virgin, this little offering of my slavery, in honor of, and in union with, that subjection which the Eternal Wisdom deigned to have to thy maternity, in homage to the power which both of you have over this poor sinner, and in thanksgiving for the privileges with which the Holy Trinity has favored thee. I declare that I wish henceforth, as thy true slave, to seek thy honor and to obey thee in all things.

O admirable Mother, present me to thy dear Son as His eternal slave, so that as He has redeemed me by thee, by thee He may receive me! O Mother of mercy, grant me the grace to obtain the true Wisdom of God; and for that end receive among those whom thou lovest and teachest, whom thou lead, nourishes and protects as thy children and thy slaves.

O faithful Virgin, make me in all things so perfect a disciple. imitator and slave of the Incarnate Wisdom, Jesus Christ thy Son, that I may attain, by thine intercession and by thine example, to the fullness of His age on earth and of His glory in Heaven. Amen.

(A plenary indulgence, under the usual conditions, on the feast of the

Immaculate Conception and April 28. Preces et Pia Opera. 75.)
"Jesus, Mary, I love You, Save Souls."

Catena Legionis

Antiphon. - Who is she that cometh forth as the morning rising, fair as the moon, bright as the Sun, terrible as an army set in battle array?

My soul doth magnify the Lord.

And my spirit hath rejoiced in God my Savior.

Because He hath regarded the humility of His handmaid: for behold from henceforth all generations shall call me blessed.

For He that is mighty hath done great things to me, and holy is His name.

And His mercy is from generation unto generations to them that fear Him.

He hath showed might in His arm: He hath scattered the proud in the conceit of their heart.

He hath put down the mighty from their seat: and hath exalted the humble.

He hath filled the hungry with good things: and the rich He hath sent empty away.

He hath received Israel His servant: being mindful of His mercy.

As He spoke to our fathers: to Abraham and to his seed forever.

Glory be to the Father, and to the Son, and to the Holy Ghost.

As it was in the beginning, is now, and ever shall be, world without end. Amen.

Antiphon. - Who is she that cometh forth as the morning rising, fair as the moon, bright as the sun, terrible as an army set in battle array?

V. O Mary conceived without sin.

R. Pray for us who have recourse to Thee.

Let us pray

O Lord Jesus Christ our Mediator with the Father, who hast been pleased to appoint the Most Blessed Virgin, Thy Mother, to be our Mother also, and our Mediatrix with Thee, mercifully grant that whosoever comes to Thee seeking Thy favors may rejoice to receive all of them through her. Amen.

"Jesus, Mary, I love You, Save Souls."

A Prayer for Priests

Keep them, I pray Thee, dearest Lord. Keep them, for they are Thine
Thy priests whose lives burn out before Thy consecrated shrine.
Keep them, for they are in the world, though from the world apart;
When earthy pleasures tempt, allure, --- shelter them in Thy heart.
Keep them, and comfort them in hours of loneliness and pain.
When all their life of sacrifice for souls seem but in vain, keep them, and O
remember, Lord, they have no one but Thee.
Yet they have only human hearts, with human frailty.
Keep them as spotless as the Host, that daily they caress;
Their every thought and word and deed, deign, dearest Lord, to bless.

Imprimatur: +D. Card. Dougherty, Arch. of Philadelphia
Our Father Hail Mary, Queen of the Clergy, pray for them.
The Priesthood Is a Masterpiece Of
Christ's Divine Love, Wisdom and Power
NEVER ATTACK A PRIEST
"Jesus, Mary, I love You, Save Souls."

CRITICISM OF PRIESTS

Our Lord's revelations to Mutter Vogel
"One should **NEVER** attack a priest, even when he's in error, rather one
should pray and do penance that I'll grant him My grace again. He alone
fully represents Me, even when he doesn't live after My example!" (page 29,
Mutter Vogel's Worldwide Love, St. Grignion Publishing House, Altoting,
South Germany (29. 6. 1929)).
When a Priest falls we should extend him a helping hand **THROUGH
PRAYER AND NOT THROUGH ATTACKS!** "I myself will be his
judge, **NO ONE BUT I!**" "Whoever voices judgment over a priest has
voiced it over Me; child, never let a Priest be attacked, take up his defense."
(Feast of Christ the King 1937)" Child, never judge your confessor, rather
pray much for him and offer every Thursday, through the hands of My
Blessed Mother, Holy Communion (for Him) (18.6. 1939)&nsp; "Never
again accept an out-of-the-way word about a Priest, and speak no unkind
word (about them) **EVEN IF IT WERE TRUE!** Every Priest is My
Vicar and My heart will be sickened and insulted because of it! If you hear
a judgment (against a Priest) pray a Hail Mary." (28. 6. 1939)
"If you see a Priest who celebrates the Holy Mass unworthily then say
nothing about him, rather tell it to Me alone! I stand beside him on the
altar!" "Oh pray much for My priests, that they'll love purity above all, that
they'll celebrate the Holy Sacrifice of the Mass with pure hands and heart.

Certainly, the Holy Sacrifice is one and the same even when it is celebrated by an unworthy priest, but the graces called down upon the people is not the same!" (28. 2. 1938)

Mary. Queen of the Clergy, pray for them.
Litany of Humility
(for private devotion only)

Which His Eminence Cardinal Merry del Val was accustomed to reciting daily after the celebration of Holy Mass.

O Jesus! meek and humble of heart, **Hear me.**
From the desire of being esteemed,
Deliver me, Jesus.
From the desire of being loved...
From the desire of being extolled ...
From the desire of being honored ...
From the desire of being praised ...
From the desire of being preferred to others...
From the desire of being consulted ...
From the desire of being approved ...
From the fear of being humiliated ...
From the fear of being despised...
From the fear of suffering rebukes ...
From the fear of being calumniated ...
From the fear of being forgotten ...
From the fear of being ridiculed ...
From the fear of being wronged ...
From the fear of being suspected ...
That others may be loved more than I,
Jesus, grant me the grace to desire it.
That others may be esteemed more than I ...
That, in the opinion of the world,
others may increase and I may decrease ...
That others may be chosen and I set aside ...
That others may be praised and I unnoticed ...
That others may be preferred to me in everything...
That others may become holier than I, provided that I may become as holy as I should
Jesus, grant me the grace to desire it

Imprimatur: + James A. McNulty - Bishop of Paterson, N.J.

11. Prayer to The Sacred Head of Our Blessed Lord

As the Seat of Divine Wisdom.
WISDOM of the Sacred Head guide me in all my ways.
O Love of the Sacred Heart, consume me with Thy fire.
Three Gloria's, in honor of the Divine Will, Memory and Understanding.
O Seat of Divine Wisdom, and guiding Power, which governs all the
motions and love of the Sacred Heart, may all minds know Thee all hearts
love Thee and all tongues praise Thee, now and for evermore.

Litany to The Sacred Head of Jesus

Lord, Have Mercy on Us Christ, Have Mercy on Us.
  Lord Have Mercy on Us
Jesus, Graciously Hear Us.
God the Father of Heaven, Have Mercy on Us.
God the Son Redeemer of the World, Have Mercy on Us.
God the Holy Ghost, Have Mercy on Us.
Sacred Head of Jesus Formed by the Holy Ghost in the Womb of the
Virgin Mary
  (after each invocation say "GUIDE US IN ALL OUR WAYS")

Sacred Head of Jesus Substantially United to the Word of God,
Sacred Head of Jesus Temple of Divine Wisdom,
Sacred Head of Jesus, Centre of Eternal Light,
Sacred Head of Jesus Tabernacle of Divine Knowledge,
Sacred Head of Jesus Safeguard Against Error,
Sacred Head of Jesus Sunshine of Heaven and Earth,
Sacred Head of Jesus Treasure of Science and Pledge of Faith,
Sacred Head of Jesus Radiant With Beauty and Justice and Love,
Sacred Head of Jesus Full of Grace and Truth,
Sacred Head of Jesus Living Witness of Humility,
Sacred Head of Jesus Reflecting the Infinite Majesty of God,

Sacred Head of Jesus Centre of the Universe,
Sacred Head of Jesus Object of the Father's Joyous Satisfaction,
Sacred Head of Jesus Upon Which the Holy Ghost Rested,
Sacred Head of Jesus Around Which the Glory of Mt. labor Shown,
Sacred Head of Jesus Who Had No Place on Earth on Which to Rest,
Sacred Head of Jesus Whom the Fragrant Anointing of Magdalen Consoled,
Sacred Head of Jesus Bathed With the Sweat of Blood in Gethsemani,
Sacred Head of Jesus who Wept for Our Sins,
Sacred Head of Jesus Crowned With Thorns,
Sacred Head of Jesus Outraged by the Indignities of the Passion,
Sacred Head of Jesus Consoled by the Loving Gesture of Veronica
Sacred Head of Jesus Bowed to the Earth Which was Redeemed
    at the Moment of Death on Calvary,
Sacred Head of Jesus Light of Every Being Born on Earth,
Sacred Head of Jesus Our Guide and Our Hope,
Sacred Head of Jesus Who Knows All our Needs,
Sacred Head of Jesus Who Gives Us All Graces,
Sacred Head of Jesus That Governs All the Motions of the Sacred Heart,
Sacred Head of Jesus Whom we Wish to Adore and Make Known
    Throughout the World,
Sacred Head of Jesus Who Knows All the Secrets of Our Hearts,
Sacred Head of Jesus Who Enraptures Angels and the Saints,
Sacred Head of Jesus Whom One Day We Hope to Behold Unveiled for Ever,
Jesus, We Adore Your Sacred Head; We Surrender Utterly to All the Decrees of Your Infinite Wisdom.

Efficacious Novena to The Sacred Heart of Jesus

I. O my Jesus, you said "verily I say to You, ask and you shall receive, seek and you shall find, knock and it shall be opened to you", behold I knock, I seek and I ask for the grace of ...

Our Father, Hail Mary, Glory be to the Father.
Sacred Heart of Jesus I put all my trust in Thee.

II. - O my Jesus, you said, "verily I say to You, whatsoever you shall ask the Father in My name, He will give it to you, behold in your name I ask the Father for the grace of...
Our Father, Hail Mary, Glory be to the Father. Sacred Heart of Jesus, I put all my trust in Thee.

III. - O my Jesus, you said, "verily I say to You, heaven and earth shall pass away but My words shall not pass away", behold I encouraged by your infallible words, now ask for the grace of...

Our Father, Hail Mary, Glory be to the Father.
Sacred Heart of Jesus, I put all my trust in Thee.

O Sacred Heart of Jesus, to whom one thing alone is impossible, namely, not to have compassion on the afflicted, have pity on us miserable sinners and grant us the grace which we ask of Thee through the Sorrowful and Immaculate Heart of Mary, your and our tender Mother.
Say the Salve Regina and add, St. Joseph, foster father of Jesus, pray for us.

P.S. - This novena prayer was recited every day by Padre Pio for all those who recommended themselves to his prayers.

Consecrating the Last Two Hours of Our Life to The Most Holy Virgin
by the late
Rev. Fr. Ildefonso M. Izaguirre, O. P.

Prostrated at thy feet, and humiliated by my sins, but full of confidence in thee, O Mary! I beg thee to accept the petition my heart is about to make. It is for my last moments. Dear Mother I wish to request thy protection and maternal love so that in the decisive instant that thou wilt do all thy love can suggest in my behalf.
To thee, O Mother of my soul, I consecrate THE LAST TWO HOURS of my life. Come to my side to receive my last breath and when death has cut the thread of my days, tell Jesus, presenting to Him my soul, "I LOVE IT". That word alone will be enough to procure for me the benediction of my God and the happiness of seeing thee for all eternity.
I put my trust in thee, my Mother and hope it will not be in vain.
O Mary! Pray for thy child and lead him to Jesus!
Amen.

"Abandoning the Mother is but one step from abandoning the Son"

Angel of God,
my guardian dear,
To whom God's love
commits me here,
Ever this day,
be at my side,
To light and guard,
Rule and guide.
Amen.

"Say daily upon arising, 7 Glory Be's to your guardian angel."

"From infancy to death human life is surrounded by their (the angels) watchful care and intercession. Beside each believer stands an angel as protector and shepherd leading him to life. Already here on earth the Christian life shares by faith in the blessed company of angels and men united to God."
- from the Catechism of the Catholic Church; 336.

10863110R00042

Printed in Great Britain
by Amazon